WHERE WE GATHER

WE GATHER AT A BUDDHIST TEMPLE

A Place in Our Community

by Sarah Shey

PEBBLE
a capstone imprint

Published by Pebble, an imprint of Capstone
1710 Roe Crest Drive, North Mankato, Minnesota 56003
capstonepub.com

Copyright © 2026 by Pebble, a Capstone imprint. All rights reserved. No part of this publication may be reproduced in whole or in part, or stored in a retrieval system, or transmitted in any form or by any means, electronic, mechanical, photocopying, recording, or otherwise, without written permission of the publisher.

Library of Congress Cataloging-in-Publication Data is available on the Library of Congress website.
ISBN: 9798875222924 (hardcover)
ISBN: 9798875222870 (paperback)
ISBN; 9798875222887 (ebook PDF)

Summary: Buddhist temples are places to pray and places to learn. Readers find out who meets at a temple, what the inside of a temple looks like, and what makes it a unique space.

Editorial Credits
Designer: Sarah Bennett; Media Researcher: Svetlana Zhurkin; Production Specialist: Tori Abraham

Image Credits
Getty Images: Aleksandr Zubkov, 21, iStock/EyeEm Mobile GmbH, 17, iStock/pilesasmiles, 8, recep-bg, 19, Vicky_bennett, 18; Shutterstock: Anirut Thailand, 14, cowardlion, cover, Cyrille Redor, 5, Guillaume Angleraud, 20, Holger Kleine, 6, kampol Jongmeesuk, 10, Karasev Viktor, 16, kizuuuneko, design element (throughout), lemaret pierrick, 13, Maximum Exposure PR, 12, Rich T Photo, 7, Sean Pavone, 9, The Road Provides, 15, urdrunkgohome, 4, Victor Jiang, 11

Any additional websites and resources referenced in this book are not maintained, authorized, or sponsored by Capstone. All product and company names are trademarks™ or registered® trademarks of their respective holders.

Printed and bound in China. 6274

Table of Contents

What Is a Buddhist Temple? 4

What's Inside? 8

Sit and Pray 16

Make an International
Buddhist Flag 20

Glossary 22

Read More 23

Internet Sites 23

Index 24

About the Author 24

Words in **bold** are in the glossary.

What Is a Buddhist Temple?

Buddhism is the world's fourth-largest religion. It is based on the teachings of the Buddha. He lived about 2,600 years ago. People who practice Buddhism are called Buddhists.

Buddhism is a huge part of the culture in Thailand.

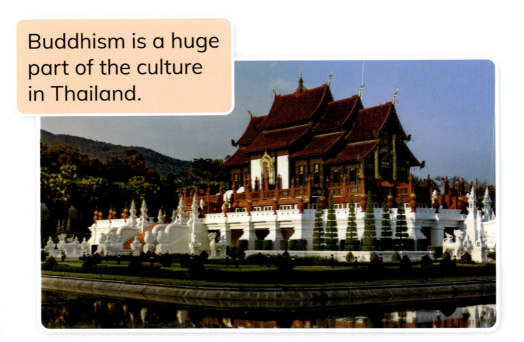

A temple in Bhutan

Buddhists pray at home or at temples. Temples can be huge or small. It does not matter what they look like. They are places of peace and reflection. All temples bring people closer to Buddha.

Signs, lanterns, and flags are in front of a temple. There might be a gate. The Three Jewels of Buddhism are there too. They represent Buddha, his teachings, and the community.

Lanterns light the way to Buddha's teachings.

A large Buddhist temple with curved roofs in South Africa

Many temples have roofs that curve up. Curves help keep rainwater away. They also are believed to push away bad spirits.

What's Inside?

Temple visitors remove hats and shoes at the door. They speak quietly and respectfully before entering the **shrine** room.

Removing your shoes before entering a temple or another person's home is a sign of respect.

Shrine rooms are sacred spaces.

Red and gold are everywhere. Red protects, and gold symbolizes goodness and compassion. There are burning candles or **incense**. There are also offerings of flowers, fruit, and water.

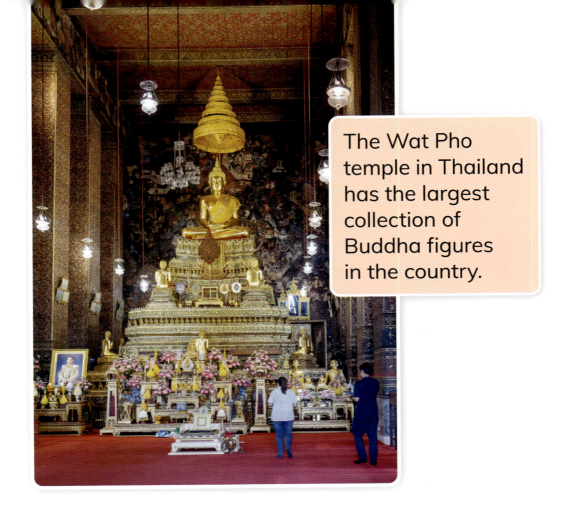

The Wat Pho temple in Thailand has the largest collection of Buddha figures in the country.

The temple's main Buddha statue sits on a center **altar**. It is surrounded by smaller Buddhas. The Buddhas remind people that they can reach **enlightenment**, just like Buddha did.

An altar in the Temple of the Sacred Tooth Relic in Sri Lanka has carvings.

Altars can be carved or painted with symbols and scenes from Buddha's life. Common symbols are lions, deer, elephants, dragons, and lotus flowers.

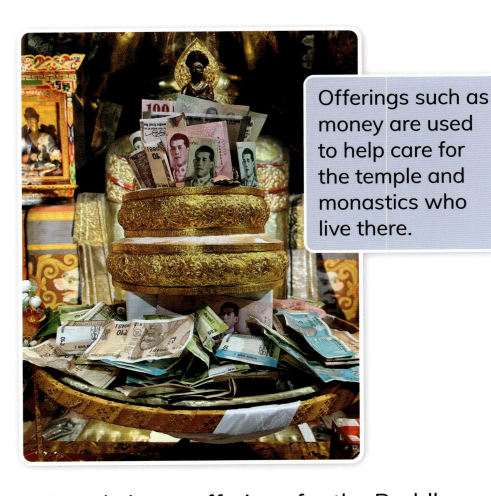

Offerings such as money are used to help care for the temple and monastics who live there.

People leave offerings for the Buddha. There are also donation boxes. Some temples have **monastics**. Monastics lead ceremonies. They also care for the temple. Donations help them spend time in prayer.

Some temples have bell-shaped **stupas**. Stupas protect important **relics**. People pray by walking around the stupa three times.

Stupas are important to Buddhists.

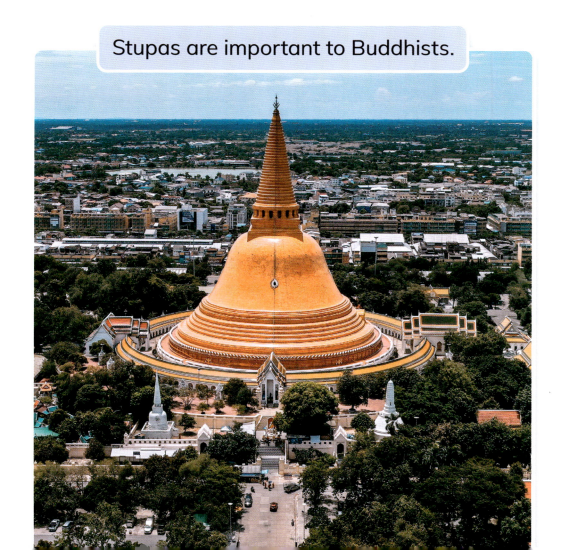

13

Meditation encourages people to relax their minds and bodies.

Larger temples have halls for meditation and teaching. There are cushions and prayer books for people to use. Monastics sit on a platform called a dais. They accept daily offerings.

People also visit the temple to learn. Some temples have classrooms and libraries. Others have kitchens. Making and sharing food is important.

Generosity is an important part of Buddhism.

Sit and Pray

Temples are open daily. People take part in chants. They meditate. Blessings are given for births, birthdays, and weddings. Visiting monastics or **lamas** give talks.

People from around the world travel to visit temples.

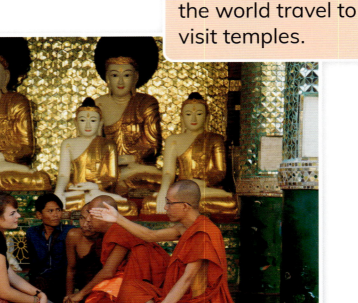

Weekends are the busiest time at Buddhist temples.

The largest crowds gather on holy days and festivals. These are times to reflect and be with family.

In some countries, children serve as novice monastics for a short time.

Some Buddhists live far from their birth country. Temples feel like home. People take language, dance, and yoga classes. They join book and gardening clubs.

18

The Buddha helped people suffer less. Buddhist temples offer ways to find peace on the path with Buddha.

Temples offer peaceful spaces to pray and feel calm.

Make an International Buddhist Flag

The International Buddhist Flag is flown at many temples. The six stripes in the flag teach about Buddha. The blue stripe represents kindness. Yellow is balance, and red is blessings. White signifies peace, and orange is wisdom.

The sixth stripe includes all five colors and represents unity. Now that you know what each color means, you can create your own flag.

What You Need

- white paper
- ruler
- pencil
- crayons or markers

What You Do

1. Lay your paper so that the longest sides are the top and bottom. With an adult's help, measure out six even stripes from top to bottom on the piece of paper.

2. Divide the last stripe into five even stripes going across.

3. Color your flag!

Glossary

altar (AHL-tuhr)—a table or platform to hold and present religious offerings

enlightenment (en-LIE-tuhn-mehnt)—the experience of awakening to reality

incense (IN-sens)—material that produces a strong smell when burned

lama (LAH-mah)—a religious teacher of Tibetan Buddhism

monastic (meh-NA-stik)—a person who carries out religious work

relic (re-LIK)—a spiritual object or fragment placed in the center of a stupa

shrine (SHRINE)—a room in a temple for prayer and reflection of Buddha and his teachings

stupa (STOO-peh)—a bell-shaped structure that serves as a Buddhist shrine

Read More

Andrews, Elizabeth. *Bon Festival*. Minneapolis: DiscoverRoo, an imprint of Pop!, 2024.

Shey, Sarah. *Buddhist Festivals and Traditions*. North Mankato, MN: Capstone, 2025.

Vallepur, Shalini. *Temple*. New York: Lightbox Learning Inc., 2024.

Internet Sites

Buddhism for Kids
buddhistchurchesofamerica.org/buddhism-for-kids

Facts About Buddhism for Kids
buddhismforkids.net/facts.html

Kiddle: Buddhism Facts for Kids
kids.kiddle.co/Buddhism

Index

altars, 10, 11

enlightenment, 10

food, 9, 15

lamas, 16

meditating, 14, 16

monastics, 12, 14, 16, 18

offerings, 9, 12, 14

relics, 13

roofs, 7

shrine rooms, 8, 9

stupas, 13

Three Jewels of Buddhism, 6

About the Author

Sarah Shey is a writer and a librarian. She is grateful to all the Buddhists who so generously agreed to be interviewed. While Buddhism has influenced her life, Shey respectfully acknowledges that she is only a cultural mediator between Buddhism and the readers of this book.